WORLD STORIES ENCYCLOPEDIA

100

AMAZING FACTS ABOUT FOOTBALL

THE BEST AMERICAN FOOTBALL TRIVIA BOOK EVER

PRESENTATION

THIS BOOK IS PART OF **THE WORLD STORIES ENCYCLOPEDIA** SERIES, AN IMPORTANT ITALIAN-AMERICAN PUBLISHING PROJECT SPECIALIZED IN PUBLICATIONS FOR CHILDREN AND YOUNG PEOPLE.

THE SERIES INCLUDES VARIOUS BOOKS WITH A FASCINATING SELECTION OF AMAZING STORIES, FACTS AND CURIOSITIES **ABOUT FOOTBALL, VARIOUS SPORTS, ANIMALS, NATURE, SCIENCE.**

ALL WITH THE HELP AND ADVICE OF EXPERTS IN THE SECTOR TO ALWAYS PROVIDE HIGH-QUALITY INFORMATION AND CONTENT.

WHAT IS EVEN MORE ATTRACTIVE IS THAT THROUGH THESE BOOKS CHILDREN AND YOUNG PEOPLE WILL PERFECT THEIR KNOWLEDGE AND LOGICAL CAPABILITIES SIMPLY HAVING FUN.
WHAT'S MORE BEAUTIFUL?

GOOD READING AND ENJOY FRIENDS.

It was November 6, 1869 when the first official American football match was played, the version of rugby with stars and stripes.

The meeting took place in New Brunswick (New Jersey), between the university teams of Rutgers and Princeton, and there were just one hundred spectators applauding them, the only eyewitnesses of a sporting event with historical significance.

It was the first of three meetings between the two university teams, which, however, was never completed. The first game was won by Rutgers 6-4, the second was won by Princeton which then, due to the refusal of the opponents to play the third match, won the victory of the mini-tournament.

These days, American football is played in public schools, colleges, and on the professional circuit. On the latter, it is a sport that generates a large amount of cash for the leagues that compete in it.

The playing field for the game is 360 yards, and the width is 160 yards. The end zones are 10 yards long, and players must wear various protective gear, including helmets, face masks, shoulder pads, thigh pads, and mouth guards. The length of the end zones is ten yards.

At the collegiate and professional levels, games are played for sixty minutes and divided into four quarters, each of which lasts fifteen minutes. A single match could last between two and a half to three hours, or even more, due to the frequent breaks in play during the competition. High school athletic competitions normally consist of four quarters, each lasting 12 minutes. It's possible that the length of games that younger children play could be cut down even further.

4

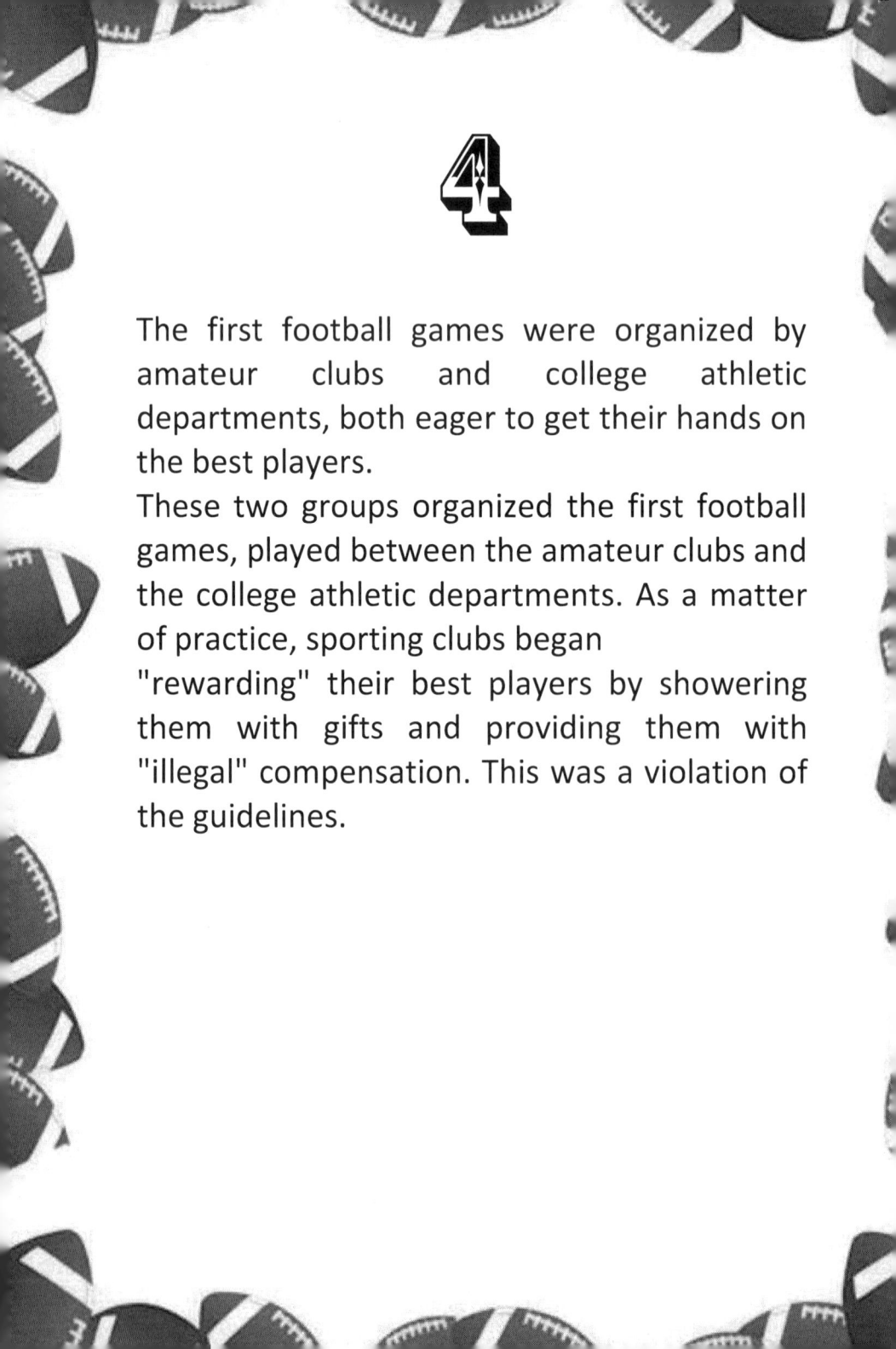

The first football games were organized by amateur clubs and college athletic departments, both eager to get their hands on the best players.

These two groups organized the first football games, played between the amateur clubs and the college athletic departments. As a matter of practice, sporting clubs began "rewarding" their best players by showering them with gifts and providing them with "illegal" compensation. This was a violation of the guidelines.

In the first ever football game, which took place on November 6, 1869, colleges Rutgers and Princeton faced off against one another. However, the rules weren't written down until the 1880s, when a superb rugby player named Walter Camp pioneered the new restrictions that revolutionized the game. This was the first time the rules had been written down. This was the very first time that the laws were committed to writing.

The American Professional Football Association was the forerunner of what would become known as the National Football League, which was established in 1920. (NFL). There are 256 games scheduled between Labor Day and New Year's Day on the National Football League's (NFL) schedule. Following the conclusion of the regular season is the postseason, which is often referred to as the playoffs. These games serve as a precursor to the Super Bowl, the title game for the NFL.

7

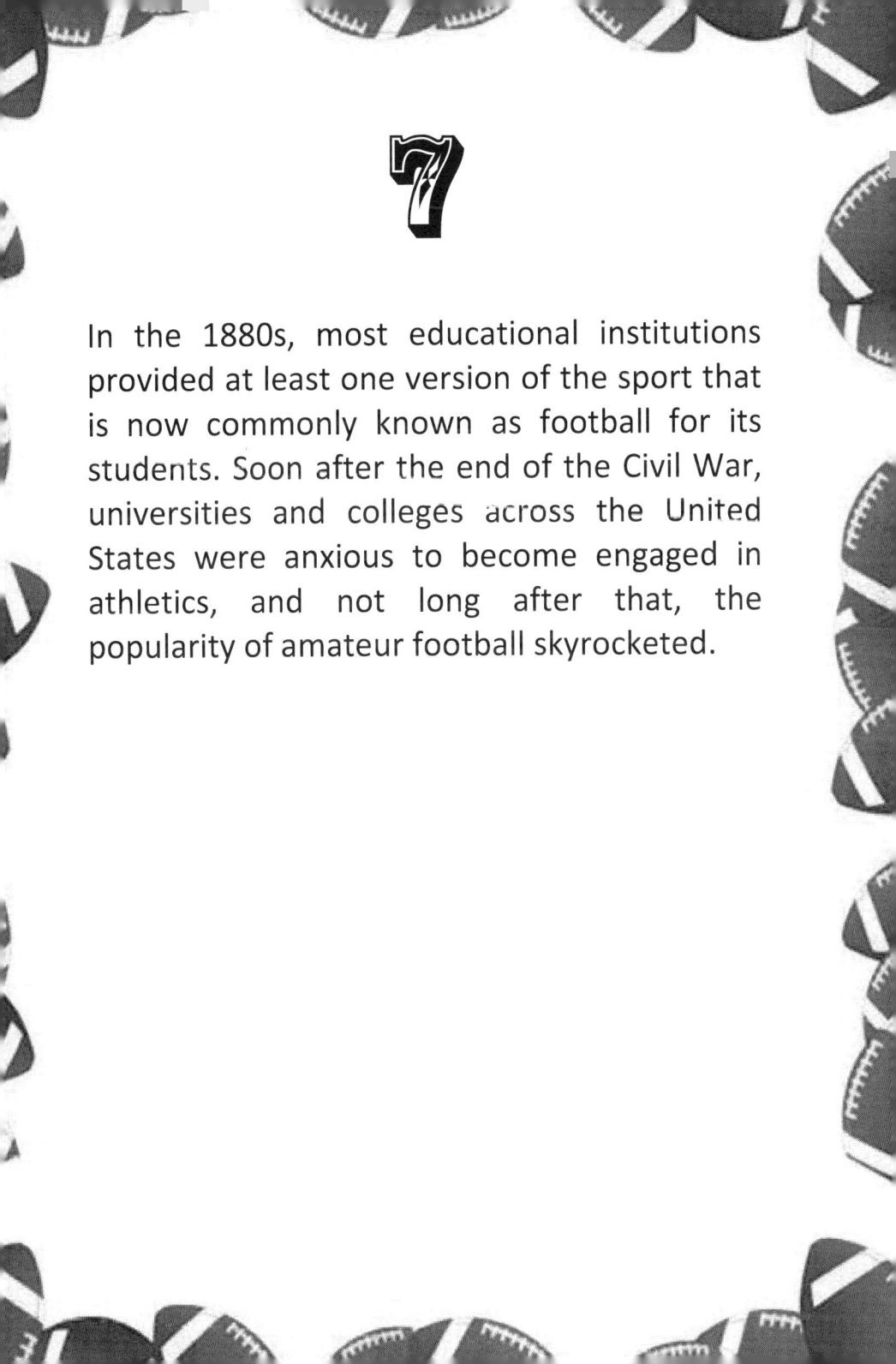

In the 1880s, most educational institutions provided at least one version of the sport that is now commonly known as football for its students. Soon after the end of the Civil War, universities and colleges across the United States were anxious to become engaged in athletics, and not long after that, the popularity of amateur football skyrocketed.

8

It used to be standard practice for amateur football clubs to "cheat" by trying to find professions for its star players outside of the sport.

Some clubs would award their best players with pricy trophies and watches, which the players would pawn or sell after each match. These trophies and timepieces were often gifts from the clubs to the players. Some organizations gave more than twice the typical amount of expense money to their best players as a form of compensation.

Although football has one of the shortest seasons of any professional sport — 17 weeks — its popularity surpasses any other sport.

This is due to tailgating, cheering for teams with stickers and flags on cars, and watching the annual Superbowl, which receives the most viewers over the entire year. Although football has one of the shortest seasons of any professional sport, it is still the most popular.

The Pittsburgh Steelers have won the most Super Bowls, as they have won six of their eight appearances in the game, making them the most successful team in Super Bowl history.

The New England Patriots and the Dallas Cowboys have participated in eight Super Bowl games; however, the Cowboys have prevailed in five of those games while the Patriots have won just four.

When selecting the best college players, certain teams are given priority over others based on the results of intricate calculations used to decide the order of the draught.

Draft pick trading is something that can be done with other teams if you so choose. The team that ended the previous season with the most losses is granted draught selection preference for the upcoming season.

The wide receiver for the Atlanta Falcons, Julio Jones, continues to break records in the National Football League. Jones broke the record for the fastest player in the sport's history to acquire 10,000 receiving yards throughout their career.

He did this by accumulating the yardage in less time than the previous record holder. It has never been done before in the history of the NFL, but his average of 96.2 receiving yards per game is the highest it has ever been.

The National Football League (NFL) running title has been won by some of the most well-known athletes in the history of the sport.

There have been a total of fourteen different runners who have taken home the title of rushing champion throughout the course of the previous seventeen years. There is a Supreme Court Justice, an Oscar-winning actress, and a Rhodes Scholar on the team, and they are all among the top rushers.

Incredible as it may seem, Princeton University holds the record for the highest number of collegiate national football championships won by any school in the history of the sport.

As a result of the fact that these victories occurred in the early 1900s and the last time Princeton took first place in a championship was in 1950, the vast majority of individuals living in today's society are taken aback by the news of these accomplishments. The University of Princeton has been victorious in a total of 28 championships.

Vinny Testaverde is the only athlete in the annals of college football history to have won the Heisman Trophy, the Maxwell Trophy, the O'Brien Trophy, and the Walter Camp Award in his senior year of competition. In addition, Testaverde was the first player chosen in the overall draught for the NFL.

Steve McNair holds several records, including the record for the most passing yards in a single game with 5,799 yards, the record for the most games with over 400 yards, and the record for the most passing in a career with 14,496 yards.

All of these records were set by Steve McNair. In addition, McNair holds the record for the highest throwing yardage average per game of any quarterback in NFL history.

There will always be winners and losers in a game of football, and Prairie View College was on a losing streak that ran for 80 games at one point.

On the other hand, the college was successful at both national championships held for black colleges in
1953 and 1964, and it won both of them.

18

In 1962, CBS paid only $4.65 million for broadcast rights; meanwhile, Fox currently spends $1.15 billion per year for the NFC broadcast rights, which doesn't even include the NFL Championship game broadcast.

The money made from football continues to increase.

Professional football competition has been given the time and attention it deserves every day of the week. On Tuesday, a blizzard that moved through Pennsylvania resulted in the cancellation of all of the day's games except for one.

The game that was supposed to take place on Wednesday between Washington and New York had to be postponed so that it would no longer compete with John McCain's acceptance speech for the Republican presidential nomination. The game will now take place on Thursday. This indicated that there would not be any additional matches played on Wednesday.

The New Orleans Saints finally achieved their goal of winning the Super Bowl after 32 years of futile attempts. The team finally broke through and secured their first victory in the postseason.

The expansion teams Carolina and Jacksonville both fought for the title of their respective conferences in their respective franchises' second season.

21

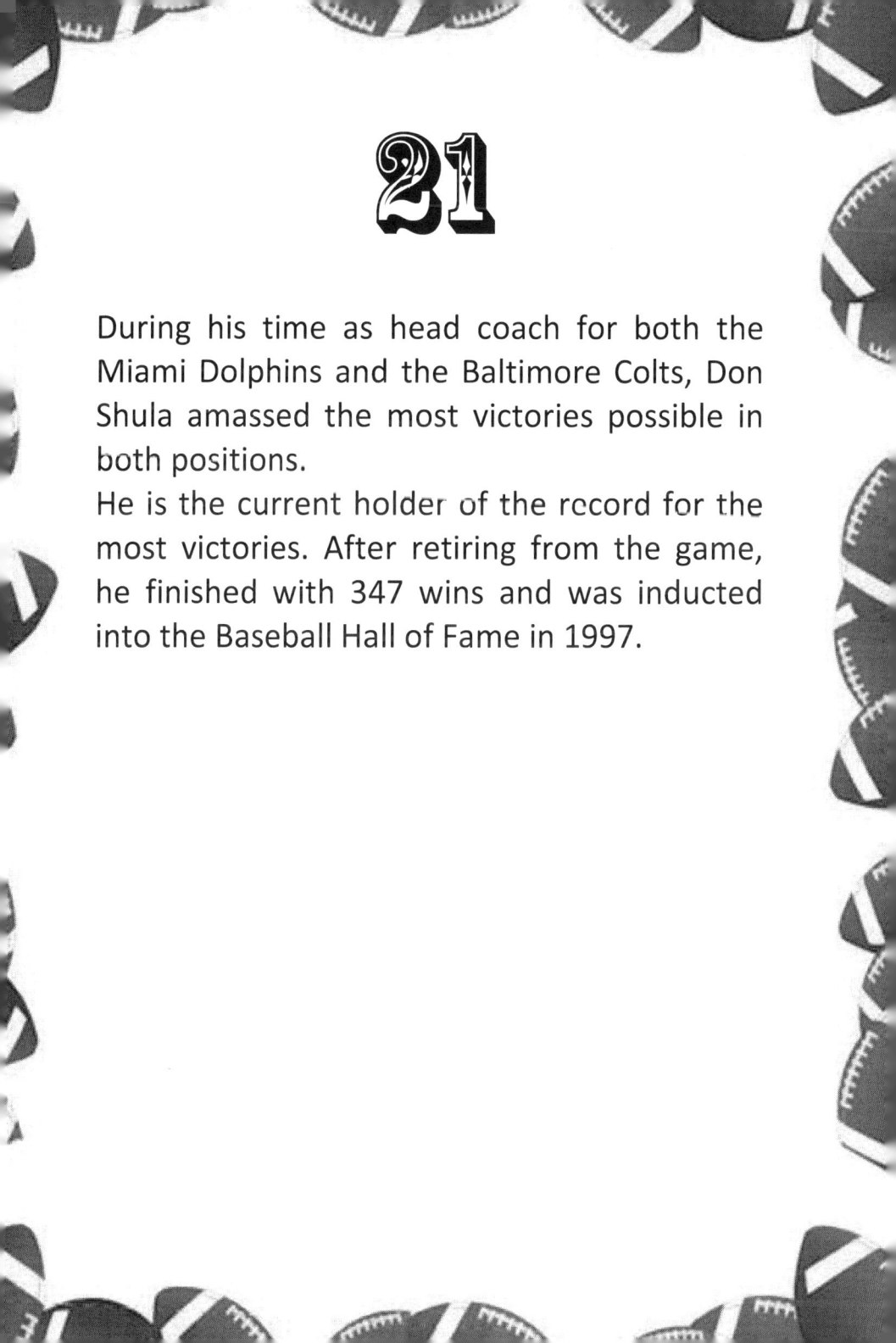

During his time as head coach for both the Miami Dolphins and the Baltimore Colts, Don Shula amassed the most victories possible in both positions.

He is the current holder of the record for the most victories. After retiring from the game, he finished with 347 wins and was inducted into the Baseball Hall of Fame in 1997.

Emmitt Smith finished his professional career with more than 18,000 yards, more than any other athlete in the history of sports has ever accumulated.

Smith's career spanned 15 years. An important aside is that Smith was crowned champion on Dancing with the Stars in 2006, which she did by winning a competition.

23

During the National Football League's (NFL) long existence, many clubs have moved to cities and states.

When the Great Depression was in its early years, moving teams did not raise as much controversy as it does now.

However, the controversy that it does cause now was not present when the Great Depression was in its early years.

The record for the highest punting average in a single season now belongs to Sammy Baugh, who achieved 51.4 yards during one of his seasons. In 1940, he established this benchmark.

Baugh's record remains unbroken; although six other players have punted for more than 50 yards in the past seven years, and nobody else has done it in the 86 years prior, Baugh's record continues to be the one that stands.

The Baltimore Ravens did not score a touchdown in five games during the season in which they won the Super Bowl in 2000. This was the season in which they also won the championship.

The club nevertheless managed to create a record for the fewest points allowed, 165, despite losing two games in the competition. The Ravens scored almost the same number of points in the Super Bowl as they did during those five notorious games.

The Houston Rockets have the unenviable reputation of being the team that has suffered the most significant decline in performance following an excellent season. In 1993, the Oilers had a terrible season, finishing with a record of 2-14 after having a record of 12-4 at the end of the previous season. In either 2012 or 2013, the team did not record a single victory in their contests.

27

In the history of the National Football League, many teams have come and gone, including the Maroons, All-Americans, Reds, Triangles, Celts, and Eskimos, to name just a few. There are many kinds of insects, such as tornadoes, marines, yellowjackets, stapes, Jeffersons, gunners, and colonels.

Many people believe that Mark Moseley, a former kicker for the Washington Redskins, is one of the most underappreciated athletes in all professional football. Moseley played for the Redskins.

He has won the same number of Most Valuable Player honors as well-known figures such as Dan Marino, Walter Payton, John Elway, Marshall Faulk, O.J. Simpson, Lawrence Taylor, Terry Bradshaw, and Emmit Smith. He has won the award ten times.

There is a widespread consensus among football fans that Brent Favre's record of 297 consecutive starts at quarterback will not be broken shortly.

Favre currently holds this record. Peyton Manning is now in second place on the list and is five seasons behind Brett Favre. Favre has led the way among quarterbacks in this category for longer. Conversely, talented quarterbacks are starting earlier in their careers, and the league is doing everything possible to protect its top players. In addition, gifted quarterbacks are starting earlier in their careers. Favre's record might slip.

The point discrepancy between two professional teams is normally not very large, and since 1987, there have been only 11 games with a point differential of 20 or more between the two teams. Although none of these underdogs have ever been victorious, the Philadelphia Eagles, a 24.5-point underdog against the New England Patriots, held the lead in the fourth quarter of their game against the Patriots before ultimately losing 31-28.

Even though none of these underdogs have ever prevailed, the Philadelphia Eagles are the only team in this group to come close to winning.

Joe Thiesman, a player for the Washington Redskins, was convinced by the director of sports information at Notre Dame to modify the way he pronounced his name from "Theez-min" to "Thighs-min" so that it would rhyme with "Heisman," the name of the coveted trophy. Jim Plunkett came out on top to win the race, while Theisman could only manage to come in second.

The idea that there was no such thing as a forward pass in early football games may surprise some people. At that time, the only method for players to advance the ball was to make their way past the line of scrimmage as quickly as possible. In its early days, football was played in a less formal environment, and teams often comprised
11, 15, 20, or 25 players. Today, the average football team has 11 players.

During a game between Yale and Princeton, Oliver Thompson scored a touchdown after Walter Camp completed a forward throw to him. The play occurred during the Yale game. It's probably not a surprise to hear that the Princeton Tigers ferociously resist it.

In the 1890s, a player named Paul Hubbard, who was deaf and relied on hand signals to communicate with his team-mates and call plays, is credited with inventing the huddle. Hubbard was a part of a squad that played American football. One tactic to prevent the opposing team from seeing their signals was having all the players congregate around the quarterback.

According to the law, William "Pudge" Heffelfinger is the first player to compete professionally in a sport. He was the first professional player to adopt a moniker and was paid $500 to play in a game in 1892. He was also the first player ever to use a nickname. He attended Yale and was a member of the college football team there during the years 1888 and 1891; both the 1888 and 1891 teams were undefeated.

He graduated from Yale in 1891. The team was only defeated twice in competition during those four years. Pudge finally earned a spot on Walter Camp's All-American team, and during his senior year at Yale, he played every single minute of every game on the schedule. In addition, Pudge was a member of the Yale squad that won the national championship.

35

1939 was significant because it was the first year professional sports were shown on television. The program did not have the same entertainment value as a modern Super Bowl game.

Only approximately 500 television sets could watch the first televised game, and the advertising did not offer anything to make people discuss it at the water cooler. The two teams competing in the game were the Brooklyn Dodgers and the Philadelphia Eagles. The entirety of the five hundred broadcast sets was stored In the city of New York.

36

There are many significant distinctions between college football and the game played at the professional level. The college balls used in the games have white stripes on each end, making it easier to see where the ball is heading while it is in motion.

37

The shape of a football is unlike any other sport, and the "pigskin" can be described most precisely as a "prolate spheroid."

Despite this, the game has achieved such a high level of popularity that the description "football-shaped" is often used to refer to the unusual shape of the object utilized in the game.

38

Even when they are very close to the top of the headlines, football games are not typically featured prominently in the media. After John F. Kennedy was assassinated, Pierre Salinger, who served as the press secretary, convinced the National Football League commissioner to resume two important games by arguing that JFK would have wanted the commissioner to do so.

The games were never shown on television, however, because of the coverage that occurred in the aftermath of the assassination and the subsequent passing of suspect Lee Harvey Oswald.

39

The huge lines of people waiting to get tickets are evidence that the Green Bay Packers have a committed fan base, which is shown by the fact that the Packers are well-known.

If you were to sign up for the waiting list for season tickets right now, there is a fair probability that it would take you close to a century before you were offered a slot. This is because there is now a very high demand for these tickets.

40

There was serious consideration given to rebranding the football team now known as the New England Patriots as either the Bay State Patriots or the BS Patriots.

They were once known as the Boston Patriots. However, after relocating to its current home in Foxborough, the team's owner decided he wanted a name more representative of the stadium's neighborhood. However, the National Football League did not like the initials, so his name was changed shortly after it was first presented.

41

The Canton Bulldogs are the reason the Pro Football Hall of Fame is located in Canton, Ohio, and if you've ever wondered why that is, the answer is that it's all because of them.

The Canton Bulldogs completed 25 games from 1921 to 1923 without picking up a single loss in the standings. In addition, Jim Thorpe was a member of the Bulldogs roster during that period.

42

Only one club in NFL history has won three consecutive titles, and it did not occur during the Super Bowl when those titles were awarded. Vince Lombardi served as that team's head coach during those years (1966–1968), and the team's name was the Green Bay Packers.

43

The kickers and punters of the National Football League typically play for a considerable amount of time throughout their careers. Jerry Rice, a wide receiver, and Brett Favre, a quarterback, are the only players who have played in more than
300 games yet are not currently playing in these positions, respectively.

44

The Dolphins and the Patriots are more well-known for having perfect regular seasons than the Chicago Bears are, although the Bears have also achieved this accomplishment twice (the first time in 1934 and the second time in 1942).

On the other hand, the Dolphins will have the privilege of moving on to a later round of the postseason than the other clubs.

45

The Chicago Bears are the team in the National Football League that has retired the most jersey numbers overall. This accomplishment puts the Bears in the lead. Even though the Dallas Cowboys and the Oakland Raiders have had a storied history, neither team honors its former players by retiring their former players' jersey numbers.

46

Most individuals who follow the National Football League know that the Buffalo Bills were unsuccessful in all four attempts to win the Super Bowl during the 1990s. This is common knowledge among those who follow the NFL. However, this does not make them the first team in history to fail to win the Super Bowl in any of their four previous attempts. The Minnesota Vikings were also successful in accomplishing this accomplishment; however, it was completed not in a row but spread out over eight years.

47

The American Professional Football Association (APFA) club that ended the 1920 season with the best overall record, as determined by winning percentage, was awarded the title of APFA champion for that year. The Akron Pros are frequently credited as being the team that won the first National Football League championship. The league's first six seasons saw four title fights for the league's championship.

The league's executive committee was in charge of mediating and settling any disputes that arose throughout these seasons.

48

On November 27, 1921, the Chicago Bears and the Green Bay Packers played each other in a football game for the very first time. The match between the Bears and the Packers was 20-0, and the Bears came out on top.

Back then, the Bears were known as the Staleys. Some people claim that the Bears' rivalry with the Packers is the oldest in the league, while others hold that the Bears' rivalry with the Cardinals has the honor of being the oldest in the company. In the all-time matchup between the Packers and the Bears, the Packers currently hold a lead of 97–95–6.

49

The term "football" was initially appropriate for the sport because it was mostly played with the feet of the players. In 1869, a collegiate game was played for the first time, although fans of today probably wouldn't have been able to recognize the action. There were 25 guys on each team, and they were not allowed to touch the ball in any way. They moved closer to the target by kicking it or swiping with their hands rather than shooting at it.

50

During his time as a student at Stanford in the early 1890s, future President Herbert Hoover served as the student manager of the school's football team.

Legend has it that when Stanford and Cal first played each other on the field in 1892, there was a holdup because Hoover neglected to bring the ball with him. This caused the game to be delayed.

51

The following issue is not present in today's games: According to the professional regulations, the home team is required to have either 36 balls (for games played outside) or 24 balls (for games played inside) ready for inspection by the referee two hours before the game is scheduled to begin.

52

Fans paying close attention to the ball can distinguish between the professional and college versions. The hops used at the college level are the same size as those used at the professional level, but the ends of the college balls have white stripes painted on them.
It is believed that these markers will make locating a passed ball while it is in motion simpler.

53

Soldier Field, which can be found in the middle of the United States, is the oldest stadium dedicated to American football. Seating is arranged in a U form, and the venue can hold 74,280 spectators.

Since 1971, Soldier Field has served as the primary venue for games between the Chicago Bears and the National Football League. In addition to that, it features things like marching bands, marching circuses, morning services, and fireworks displays. If you are interested in learning how to purchase Liverpool tickets online, you should know that Football Ticket Pad is the best place to do so for the entire season.

54

Many kinds of food are available for the Super Bowl, including chicken wings, pizza, pretzels, chips, and nuts. Pizza and chicken wings are the most consumed appetizers during the Super Bowl.

There is a greater demand for pizza on the day of the Super Bowl than on any other day. Since pizza is a genre of cuisine that socially ties activities together (Super Bowl), on the other side, 1.25 billion chicken wings were also devoured by American people on Super Bowl Sunday.

55

In the high-flying offences of the modern day, this is particularly surprising. Indeed, the Bears haven't had a truly exceptional quarterback since Sid Luckman back in the 1940s, even teams that feel the same way, like the Cleveland Browns, have at least one quarterback on their roster.

Joe Namath's 1967 season with the New York Jets in the American Football League is the only time anyone has ever thrown for 4,000 yards. This was the very first time anyone had ever accomplished this feat.

56

In order to properly set the stage, the event took place at Franklin Field in Philadelphia on October 11th, 1959. Bert Bell, the current commissioner of the National Football League, watched a meaningless game between the Philadelphia Eagles and the Pittsburgh Steelers, two teams he owned before becoming commissioner. Now, before I tell you this next part of the narrative, I want to point out that my research into this topic has left me unsure about the order in which the events transpired. Therefore, I will present them all at the same time. Late in the fourth quarter, the Eagles' Norm Van Brocklin found Tommy MacDonald in the end zone to seal the game, and Bell suffered a fatal heart attack in the stands. Some stories claim that the touchdown caused Bell to suffer a heart attack, while others claim that the frenetic reaction of the crowd may have been what allowed the Steelers' defense to be distracted just enough to allow for the touchdown.

57

Bobby Layne, the quarterback for the Lions, was instrumental in the team's victory in the 1957 NFL Championship game, which gave the Lions their third title of the decade overall.

The following year, the Lions dealt Layne to the Steelers, and it was reported that he predicted that the Lions would not win another title for at least half a century. It's been sixty-five years since that rumoured remark, and the Lions haven't even gone close to matching their performance. They would only qualify for the playoffs three times over the next three decades, and each time they would be eliminated in the first round.

58

The NFC South is characterized by a high degree of unpredictability. The Kansas City Chiefs won the last six titles in the AFC West, followed by the Denver Broncos winning five in that division. However, this does not appear to be the case in the NFC South, where the Carolina Panthers have won the last three titles in a row. Although this may change because the New Orleans Saints have won four consecutive games from 2017-2020, it is astonishing how evenly the division is matched. The Buccaneers, of course, competed in and won Super Bowl XXXVII in 2002 and Super Bowl LV in 2020, both of which took place in Tampa Bay. The Falcons suffered their only defeat of the season in the 2016 edition of Super Bowl LI.

The Panthers could not win either of their appearances in the Super Bowl in 2015 (Super Bowl XXXVIII and Super Bowl 50). In contrast, the Saints were victorious in their only appearance
in the Super Bowl to date (Super Bowl XLIV in 2009).

59

When the team moved from Boston to Foxborough, the owners sought a name that was less specific to the city of Boston and more indicative of the surrounding area. Bay State was the first name that was suggested to the league before New England was even considered.

On the other hand, the owning group abbreviated the title to the BS Patriots, which... You should be able to understand why the NFL did not take well to that at all. As a result, the New England Patriots came into existence, and the rest, as they say, is history.

60

September 13, 1992. It was Brett Favre's first season in Green Bay, and the receiver who caught his first successful throw is the one in whom he has the utmost faith beyond all others on the earth. Himself.

The pass that Favre attempted on a rollout bootleg was intercepted by himself for a loss of seven yards after it went straight off the helmet of a Tampa Bay Buccaneer player. As a member of the Minnesota Vikings in 2009, Favre caught a pass he had thrown himself for a loss of two yards. The only other player in the history of the NFL to catch a pass after turning 40, who was he? This is Jerry Rice.

61

1982 was the year in question. The list of NFL players protesting for better treatment by owners was growing at the same time that hair was all the rage. The kicker was the standout performer In the season that was cut short due to a strike.

Imagine for a moment that this took place in the present day and that Justin Tucker was awarded MVP. Even if he kicked 95% of his field goals and had a few key field goals in the context of Washington's season, it is still inherently unusual for a kicker, of all people, to earn MVP. If you feel like you need to pinch yourself, you certainly can.

62

It is now a given that the best college football players will leave for the professional ranks after their third year of school, with juniors and redshirt sophomores being a common sight among the early picks in the draught nowadays. It is also a given that the best college football players will leave after their third year of school. However, to be eligible for the draught before 1990, you must have completed at least four years of college.

This factor made it possible for things like Archie Griffin to win back- to-back Heisman trophies at Ohio State or for an increasing number of dynasties. Consistency was of the utmost importance when you spent four years working with the same team. The game is played differently now that the transfer site, NIL money, and eligibility differences have been implemented.

63

The first American football game was played in 1869 between Rutgers University and Princeton University.

The game wasn't played for the first time until 1869, and the regulations significantly differed from the rules of the modern game we play today. After some time had passed, in the year 1880, Walter Camp was the one who first wrote the game's rules. Walter also established the number of players on each squad and the touchdown scoring method. However, his rules have been revised.

64

It Is Common Knowledge That American Football Is the Most Well-Liked Sport in the United States. Even though the season of this football game only lasts for 17 weeks, which may seem like a very small amount of time, the fact that people will always enjoy watching the game does not vary. The stadia are constantly packed with fans rooting for the teams they believe to be the best. The game is the most popular sport in the United States, and its championship and the Super Bowl are the events on television that receive the most viewers annually.

65

The National Football League (NFL) is the game's governing body in the United States. In 1920, the organization that would later become known as the National Football League (NFL) was first created. Back then, it was known as the American Professional Football Association. The National Football League monitors every play to ensure that the stipulations of the game are adhered to. They also manage the
256 games throughout the season's 17 weeks. Games often begin the week after Labor Day and continue into the beginning of the new year.

❝

The National Football League's championship game is called the Super Bowl. Each year, the winners of the National Football Conference and the American Football Conference battle against one another at the Super Bowl to determine the NFL champion.

It is consistently ranked as one of the most-watched football games in the United States. The conclusion of the football season often occurs with the Super Bowl.

67

College Football Players are Selected for Teams Via a Draft The National Football League (NFL) holds a draught each year to pick players for teams comprised of college players. Contracts are offered to young athletes that are qualified.

The side that finishes the match with the most defeats will get the first choice in the subsequent round. The order of the draught picks is determined by the number of games each team has lost, and the team that comes out on top will have the last selection.

68

AFC and NFC are the two conferences that make up the National Football League, which has 32 teams.

The National Football Conference and the American Football Conference have 16 clubs, making up the National Football League (NFL). Every year, one championship game occurs between the two conferences. The champions will then compete against one another at the Super Bowl.

69

Most individuals who watch athletic events on television in the United States choose to watch American football. This makes American football the most popular sport in the country.

By a wide margin, the most popular form of football is played at the university and professional levels. Football played at the high school, and younger levels is another significant fundamental circumstance of the game. In the United States, around 1.1 million high academy athletes and 70,000 council athletes engaged in the sport annually as of 2012.

These numbers represent the total number of athletes who competed in the sport.

70

The "Snap," the "Line of Conflict," "Eleven Player Brigades," and the Concept of Downs Were All Established Through a Set of Rule Changes Drafted Beginning in the Year 1880 by Walter Camp, Who Is Considered to Be the "Father of American Football."

The "Snap" refers to the moment the ball is passed from one team to another during a play.

The forward pass is now permitted, there is now a neutral zone, and the proportions and dimensions of the football itself have been described. These rule changes were implemented in the most recent rule modifications.

71

It's generally agreed that Canadian and American football are the two most important forms of gridiron football. Both gridiron football and American football evolved from rugby and are now played on a football field. The most common and widely played football variation in Canada is Canadian football.

There are a few notable rule differences between the two games, even though they have very similar rules.

72

In the 1880s, nearly every American fraternity and sorority held at least one game of a sport that we now refer to as football. In those days, the game was called soccer.

After the end of the Civil War, schools all over the United States were keen to include calisthenics in their curricula, and amateur football quickly became extremely popular.

73

From 1892 through 1895, Paul D. Hubbard was a student at Gallaudet University, a college for the deaf and the hard of hearing. During that period, he was also the starting quarterback for the Gallaudet University football team. Because Hubbard's team frequently utilized sign language to discuss their next play, he set out to find a way for his team to communicate using sign language but preventing the opposing side from being able to see their signals.

That is when he had the idea to assemble his teammates around him in a tight circle, which is a tradition that has been carried up to the present day until the present day itself.

74

As of the 2015-2016 NFL season, seven NFL organizations do not use a professional cheerleading group. One of these organizations is the New England Patriots. Some examples of these are included below: The clubs that compete in this division include the Cleveland Browns, the Buffalo Bills, the Pittsburgh Steelers, the New York Giants, the Green Bay Packers, Chicago Bears, and the Lions. It was the first time in the history of a championship game that cheerleaders were not present on either side of the field.

This was also the first time that this had ever happened. This took place between the Green Bay Packers and the Pittsburgh Steelers as they competed in Super Bowl XLV.

75

Over time, eating eggs and celebrating Easter have become inseparable; the same can be said of eating pizza and watching the Super Bowl on a Sunday. More Italian flatbread is sold on the day that the National Football League championship game is played in the United States than on any other day of the year combined. This is because of the popularity of the game. It was projected that Domino's alone would serve approximately 11 million slices to hungry customers in 2015, comparable to
1,500 orders being placed every minute. In addition, the business is expected to provide somewhere around 3 million chicken wings. It just so happens that today is the day of the week when the greatest number of pizza delivery drivers are hurt or killed in automobile accidents.

76

According to a report written and distributed by Business Insider in 2015, the average income of an NFL player is listed as the sixth best compared to athletes competing in other sports leagues from all over the world.

Although the average player compensation for the 2014-2015 season was $2.11 million, this amount pales in comparison to the incomes of players in the NBA, the Indian Premier League, Major League Baseball, the National Hockey League, and the European Premier League (in descending order).

77

At the beginning of the 20th century, when players did not wear pads or even leather helmets, it gave the appearance that competitors at the high school and college levels were dropping like flies. This was the case even though player safety had improved significantly. Some victims perished due to traumatic head injuries, while others succumbed to shattered backs or crushed organs. All of the victims, however, succumbed to their injuries.

It was determined that the horrifying technique known as the Flying Wedge was one of the major factors contributing to the issue; consequently, it was ruled banned on all levels. The degree of violence reached such an extreme that even the notoriously harsh President Teddy Roosevelt was compelled to call a gathering of experts and instructors to discuss how to address the problem.

78

Even though Green Bay, Wisconsin, is the smallest city in the National Football League that is home to a club, the fans there have consistently shown themselves to be the most dedicated year after year. Fans have been purchasing tickets for the forthcoming season for years in advance, and it is said that there are currently
86,000 Cheeseheads on a waiting list that only has approximately 100 slots available each year (usually when people die). Someone who gets their name on the list right now will only have to wait around 955 years, which is just enough time to watch a robot version of Roger Goodell organize a global conquest.

79

The National Football League (NFL) was founded in 1920, and from that year until 1960, it was the dominant football league in the United States. The American Football League's fourth iteration made its debut then, immediately posing a danger to the organization that was already in place concerning player contracts and broadcasting agreements.

At that time, the American Football League was in its fourth iteration. The two leagues agreed in 1966 to combine their activities due to the severity of the threat, yet, they continued to do so as two separate businesses until 1970. This was done, although they continued to do so. (although their champions would face off against each other in the first four Super Bowls)

80

During the halftime performance of the Super Bowl, millions of individuals in the United States run to the restroom to take care of some business that has been piling up for a very long time. This is because the situation has been building up for quite some time.

Consequently, it is estimated that 90 million toilets are flushed daily, which causes more than 100 million gallons of water to pass through the sewage pipelines across the country. If you were curious, the difference between the two amounts is the same as water pouring over Niagara Falls nonstop for seven minutes.

81

Shepard received the starting nod in 12 of the 13 games that the squad competed in while he was a junior in 2014. During the game against Iowa State, he was making a reception when he sustained an injury to his groyne, which caused him to be sidelined for the remainder of that game and the following week against Baylor. As a direct consequence of this, throughout the course of the remaining four games of the season, he could only make one reception for a total of 13 yards. In the first seven games of the season, he had 49 receptions, 911 yards, and five touchdowns from those grabs.

82

A study conducted in 2010 by the Wall Street Journal based on observations from four broadcasts indicated that the average time spent on actual game action during a National Football League game was only 10 minutes and 43 seconds.

The events normally last for three hours, and around one-third of it is dedicated to ads during that time. Most of the time, the networks dedicated to airing the game are spent on replays or pictures of the players huddling together.

83

According to a study conducted and published in Sports Illustrated in 2009, more than 78 percent of former National Football League players have filed for bankruptcy or are under serious financial difficulty after two years of retirement.

84

The fog was so thick during the National Football League playoff game between the Philadelphia Eagles and the Chicago Bears in 1988 that the players could not even see the sidelines, and the fans could not see the playing field. The game was played in Philadelphia. Following each play, the officials were obligated to report what had occurred in the game.

85

Deion Sanders is the first player in the history of the major leagues to hit a home run and score a touchdown in the National Football League in the same week (1989 season).

Sanders is the only male athlete in the annals of sports history to have competed in both the Super Bowl and the World Series.

86

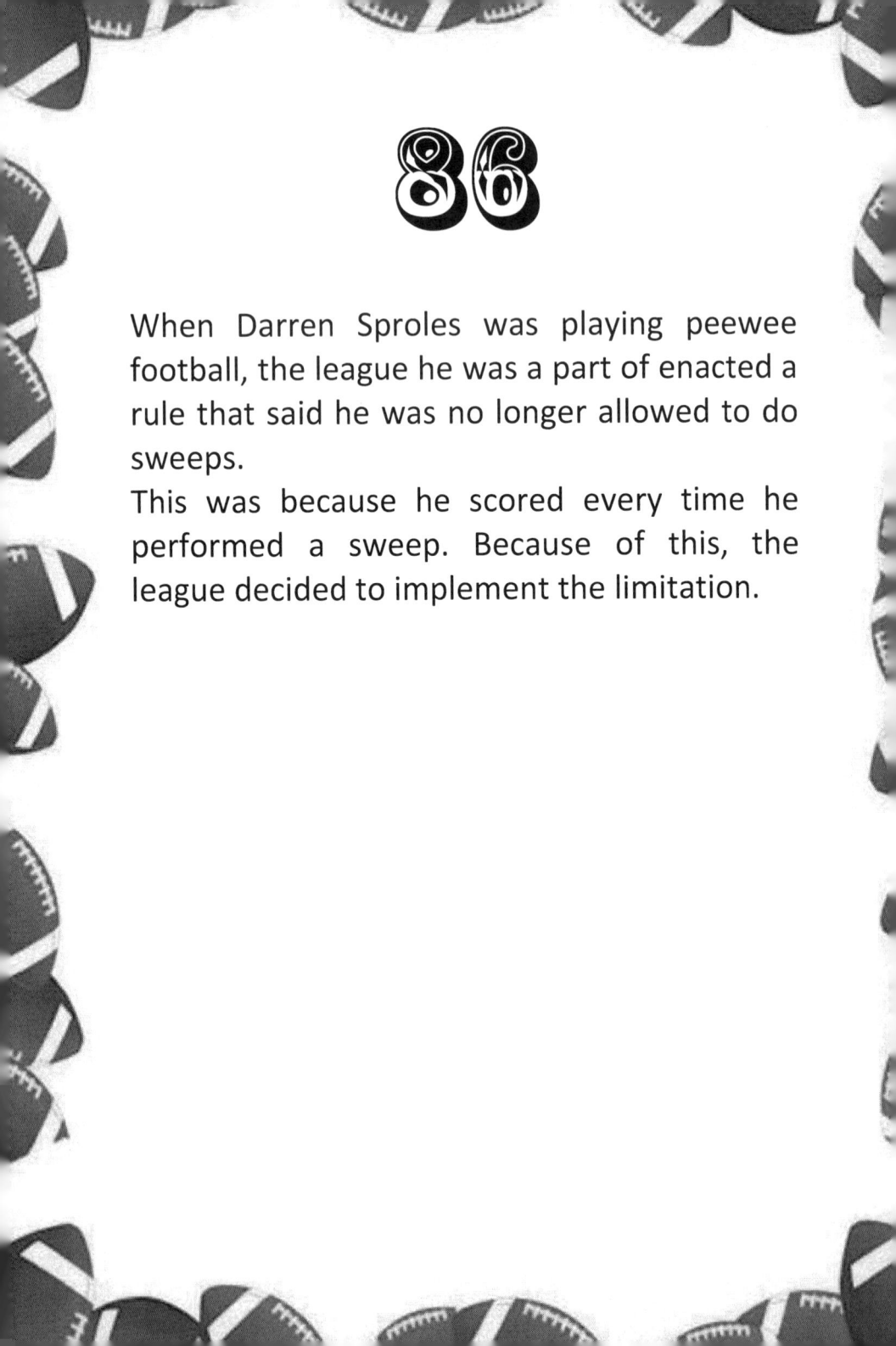

When Darren Sproles was playing peewee football, the league he was a part of enacted a rule that said he was no longer allowed to do sweeps.

This was because he scored every time he performed a sweep. Because of this, the league decided to implement the limitation.

87

The National Football League (NFL) will have a "disaster draught" if one franchise is involved in a catastrophe or is dangerously close to being destroyed.

According to the National Football League (NFL), there is a "near-disaster" when there are fewer than 15 player casualties, and there is a "disaster" when there are more than 15 player casualties. "Near-disaster" and "disaster" are both capitalized terms. Other sports leagues have rules and regulations that are very similar to these.

88

Playmakers were the title of an ESPN program broadcast on the network. It was their first attempt at producing an original drama series, and it was on the life of an American football squad.

Even though it had very strong ratings, the show was cancelled after 11 episodes because of pressure from the National Football League (NFL), which considered the show projected a negative image of professional
football players.

89

People who live within a certain distance of the stadium are required to buy tickets if they want to watch the game because certain NFL clubs won't broadcast the game if they don't sell enough tickets for their home games.

This means people within this distance must buy tickets to watch the game.

90

The National Football League championship game in 1967 was called the "Ice Bowl" by the sports media. The Green Bay Packers were victorious, defeating the Dallas Cowboys by scoring 21–17 to take the trophy.

The temperature at Lambeau Field was -15 degrees Fahrenheit when the game started, but the wind chill made it feel almost -48 degrees. It is well-known throughout the history of the National Football League as the game that was played at the coldest temperature ever recorded.

91

On April 17, 1963, NFL Commissioner Pete Rozelle stated that two players would be penalized for betting on National Football League games and associating with gamblers.
The players were defensive tackle Alex Karras of the Detroit Lions and running back Paul Hornung of the Green Bay Packers. The two players were obliged to complete the entirety of their suspensions before being allowed to return to the club.

92

The first Super Bowl to utilize Roman numerals was the fifth one, and after that, the numbers I through IV were retrospectively added back into the sequence of the previous four events. This was done so that the Roman numerals would match the order of the events. An excerpt from the National Football League's media guide reads: "The Roman numerals were adopted to clarify any confusion that may occur because the NFL Championship Game, also known as the Super Bowl, is played in the year following a chronologically recorded season." This passage is taken from the media guide for the NFL (NFL). In other words, calling the game "Super Bowl 2020" could lead to confusion because most of the season will occur in 2020, but the actual Super Bowl won't happen until 2021. The real Super Bowl won't take place until 2021.

93

It is tradition for the winning team to be presented with roughly 150 Super Bowl rings encrusted with gems. These rings are then given to the players, coaches, and other important organization members. When everything is totalled up, the collection has a value of around 5 million dollars. William "The Refrigerator" Perry
was awarded a size 25 ring for his performance with the Chicago Bears in Super Bowl XX. This ring was the largest one that had been made up until then.

94

It is customary for the Super Bowl to be played inside a stadium or at a location with a significantly warmer climate. The fourth Super Bowl, held in New Orleans' Tulane Stadium and had a temperature of 39 degrees before the game began, stands out as having the coldest playing conditions of all of the Super Bowls. The Kansas City
Chiefs were victorious over the Minnesota Vikings in that contest, taking home the trophy for their efforts.

95

In addition to the salary they get from the National Football League, players are also eligible for postseason bonuses. When all of the players' incentives from the various rounds of the playoffs up to that point were added up, the bulk of the players on the winning teams in 2021 ended up receiving a total of $250,000.

On the other hand, you shouldn't feel too sorry for the club that finished in last place because they still ended up with approximately $185,000 to spend for their postseason play. It would be best if you tried to keep your feelings in check.

96

While all the other games were played in different locations, the Buccaneers of Tampa Bay were the only team to play in their stadium. They could accomplish this by qualifying for Super Bowl LV, played at Raymond James Stadium.

This allowed them to acquire this classification. The victory in this game was their pinnacle accomplishment. On the other hand, the Rams will be playing at home this year, making it the second year in a row that the side playing at home has been victorious.

97

Four teams in the National Football League have never competed in the Super Bowl: the Detroit Lions, the Cleveland Browns, the Houston Texans, and the Jacksonville Jaguars. Having this document in your possession is quite embarrassing. It is reasonable to anticipate that none of these clubs will earn a postseason berth in
2022, given that none did so in the current season.

98

The Denver Broncos and the New England Patriots have five losses to their names due to their play in the NFL. The Broncos have a record of three wins to their name, with the most recent coming in the year 2016.

There is no possibility that the Broncos will participate in Super Bowl LVI, given that they could not earn a spot in the playoffs this season.

99

Following the break-up of NFL Europe, the National Football League (NFL) has concluded that it needs to try to grow its footprint in Europe in some other way. The NFL International Series is the name they settled on for the annual collection of games staged abroad in the United States. It is a collection of games known as the NFL International Bowl.

The league's plays have been held worldwide, including in cities such as Toronto and Mexico City, as well as the United Kingdom. The National Football League (NFL) has just lately made public its intention to enter the football markets in China and Germany relatively soon.

100

In 2007, the National Football League (NFL) concluded that it would be best to shut down NFL Europe permanently. Roger Goodell, who was just recently appointed to his position, was the one who ultimately took the choice to take action, but the plan had been in the works for a considerable amount of time before that. In 2003, several league owners made a concerted effort to have the league abolished, which came dangerously close to happening.

In the end, it was to be expected that every team in the league would fold their operations, and that's exactly what happened. On the other hand, certain teams, such as the Frankfurt Universe, have been founded to honour the founding squad in their city. This was the motivation behind the establishment of these teams.